I0186151

My Sistah's Keeper
(Keeper of words)

By
Glenda Richardson

My Sistah's Keeper
(Keeper of words)

ISBN-13: 978-0988572928

DEDICATION

I would like to dedicate this book to my children Charniece, Richard and Malik, who sat patiently as I read my poems for whatever I needed it for: A Mama G event, spoken word or just to see how something sounded. I dedicate this book to my mom Sandra Ryce who passed away April 2009 and to my Aunt Gwendolyn Moore who passed away 2018, she always encouraged me to save my early pieces. (I never did, till later.)

Lastly, I want to thank my barrage of friends, who let me bend their ear as well. They know who they are and I hope it doesn't bother them that I don't mention them individually, so as not to forget anyone. But I do thank each and every one of you and if it hadn't been for you listening and encouraging, this book would not have come about. I feel like I need to speak these words and maybe someone may want or need to hear them. Either way, here goes and I hope that this touches someone in some way.

Acknowledgment

I want to thank God for my gift of poetry writing, my mother Sandra
Ryce for giving me life, my Aunt Gwen Moore for always encouraging
me to keep writing when I was small, my children Charniece, Richard
and
Malik for always listening to me recite new pieces, that I came up with
for any occasion that I needed a poem for. I want to thank all
of my family, friends, coworkers and random strangers that listen to my
poems in the making. I didn't want to forget anyone, so I want to thank
everyone. You know who you are and how much I appreciate you
listening
to me, believing in me and my dream to at least leave my mark.

I want to give a special thank you to a dear friend: David Broussard,
who took
the time to help walk me thru every step of this process from beginning
to end. He took his time and was very patient with this entire process
and I couldn't be more grateful.

Thank you all and I hope you enjoy just a
small part of me through my poet words.

Table of Contents

"Young Black Men"

There are times,
You want to wrap your arms around them,
To keep them safe.
Other times, you know they're covered by god's grace.
I pray each day,
That you aren't singled out
Cause another's perception or views of you
Are not what you're about.
The color of your skin,
Shouldn't diminish the worth of your life.
Because living each day is already a struggle or a plight.
My heart goes out, to our young men of today
And to their families who constantly have to worry and to pray,
That they return home safely at the end of the day.
Things really haven't changed much from way back when
They're just cooking it up differently
And serving it up again.

"To Make Ends Meet"

Working hard
To make ends meet
You jump out of bed and free from the sheets.
Little food in your stomach, yet your feet hit the streets.
To get your hustle on, you're ready to go
You've made a few hustles and you need a few mo.
When you come home at the end of the day
Calculating your bills, but the same they stay.
Working hard
To make ends meet
You feed the kids, but you don't eat.
You rob Peter to pay Paul
When all's said and done
Nothing's resolved
When you get a shut off notice, what do you do
You call up a friend
That you hope will spot you.
Tomorrow is yet another day
So another hustle paves the way.
No one to blame, no need to complain
Just work much harder to make a change.
Working hard
To make ends meet
If you work in an office or out on the streets
Our needs are all the same
To make ends meet
To ease the strain

"Why Does Your Mother Cry For You?"

Why does your mother cry for you, she cries because she's sad
She's sad because she's given you, all that she had
She knows you turned out different, from what she wanted you to be
But still she loves you, and this you couldn't see
You were taken over by the drugs, that called you by name
Bringing your mother, nothing but pain.
Still she loved you, with all of her heart
Hoping that one day, the drugs and you would part.
Why does your mother cry for you, because she doesn't want to see
The frightening reality, that may one day come true.
That's when she has to come
Identify
And then to bury you.

"Momma Don't Cry"

Momma don't cry, I didn't mean to hurt you

I would never intentionally, leave and desert you.

Please forgive me, I know not what I do

But what I do know is, I didn't mean you hurt you.

To see the tears in your eyes, fill me with great shame

I know what i do is wrong, but it takes away the pain.

You may not know this, but now I think I'll share

No love could compare to yours, but you were never there.

You clothed and you kept me fed

But there was a void, I needed filled instead

I know it's in a mother's nature, to worry all the time

But momma don't cry, I'll be just fine!

"Take Some Time"

Sometimes we take life far too seriously
I'm sure that's not how, it's supposed to be.
We need to stop for a minute
And simply look around
We might even be surprised
By what's really going down.
With a second glance
You might even be enchanted
By some of the small things
We often take for granted
We can use our hands
To lace and tie our shoes
We can use our mouth
To voice and express our views
We can use our eyes
To watch the sunset each day
We can even use our ears
To listen to children play
So why be in such a hurry
And not lend a helping hand
Because we all had to crawl before we could stand
Don't be in such a hurry to look the other way
Because it may be you, in need of help one day
And don't be so eager to kick someone when their down
Because you know what they say
What goes around comes around!

"Together"

We were brought here together
In this endless love affair
I wasn't lookin for love
You just happen to be there.

We've had good times and bad times
We've had our ups and downs
But there is no one else
I'd rather be around.

You're my lover, my friend
My companion to the end
And although we argue
We always make amends.

With the love I have for you
It was like investing in fine stock
Cause our return
Is now solid as a rock.

So let's keep this thing together
Like Bonnie and Clyde
And as we grow old
Continue to enjoy the ride.

Since god has blessed us
And we are here today
I thank him for you
In every prayer that i pray

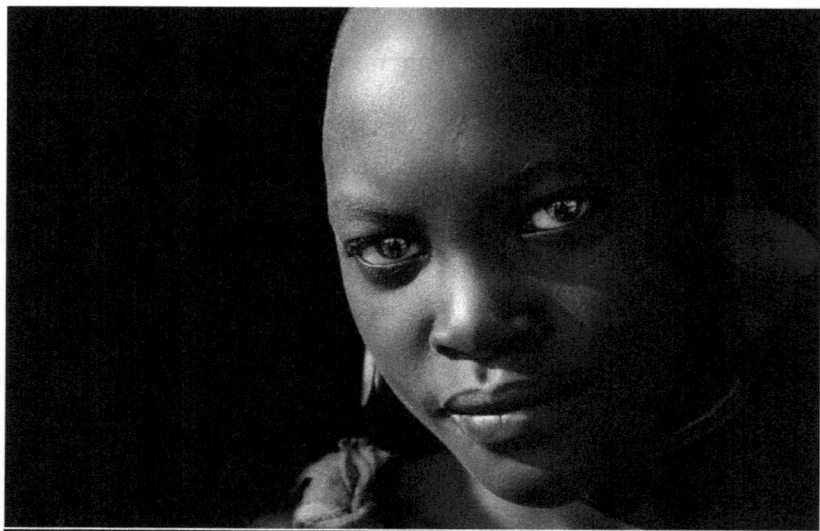

"Be Strong"

She knows, a lot has happened in her life
Often breaking her will to fight
Be she continues to be strong.
Men have said they love her and then walked away
This makes her afraid of the games they play
But she continues to be strong.
Raised with yelling, drinking and drugs
Makes her wonder what's this thing called love
But she continues to be strong.
Life has dealt her a hand so cold
It makes her feel a hundred years old
But she continues to be strong.
She's learned to better herself
Love herself and feel good about herself
Cause the only one she has to prove anything to…. Is herself
And she continues to be strong

"Women"

As women, we are unpredictable
Our attitudes can change, as the wind blows.
Sometimes there are things about us
That you'll never know
But your patience is needed
As we go with the flow.
I know you want to tend, to all of my needs.
To solve some of my problems,
Simply be there for me.
Today, it may be that I broke a nail
Tomorrow I may get some news in the mail.
Yesterday, you didn't kiss me goodbye
Then there was the issue that made me want to cry
We try to be strong and keep it together
Then there are times, we can't fare the weather.
When you have that someone
Who truly has your back
There isn't anything that can really top that.
That person whose pockets aren't necessarily filled
But he is that one, who always keeps it real.

"Caught Up"

Why do people get caught up
Blackmailed by another for a buck
If you have a secret that you don't tell
You can rest assure, it could cause you hell.
Don't be so ashamed that you get caught up
Because one pay day will never be enough
You might regret what it is you did
But some things may never stay hid.
Don't give anyone power over you
Just come clean before they do.
Cause me, myself, I don't have a dime
And blackmail is a complete waste of time.

"Violated"

What are you supposed to do
When a stranger is laying on top of you.
He doesn't seem to care
If you're a mother or a wife
Just that if you scream
He will take your life.
It happened to her
But it wasn't her fault.
She was the victim, of a vicious gang assault.
How can you take something
That doesn't belong to you
Then threaten to do harm,
When you do what you do.
How can they hurt someone
And violate them in every way
Never giving thought
To how things could change one day.
Think long and hard
About what it is you do
Because when you end up in prison
Guess who violates who?

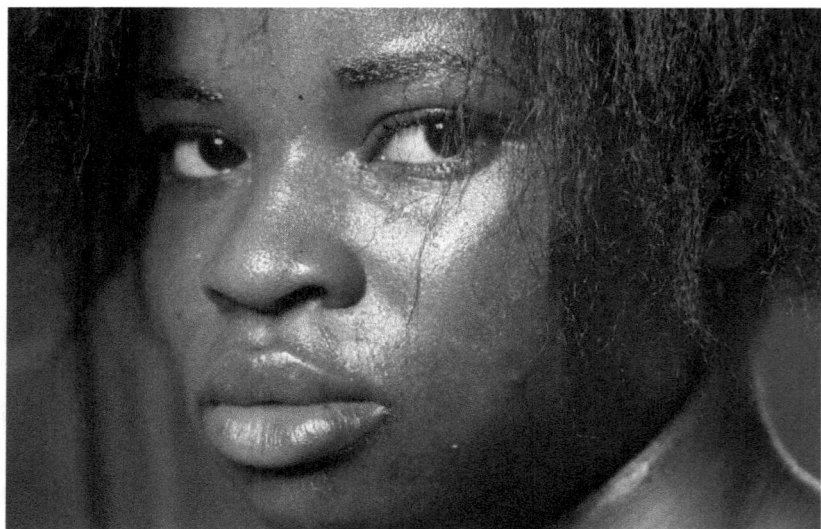

"When A Man Abuses A Woman"

When a man abuses a woman
He will often apologize
But it's treatment that he needs
But he doesn't realize.

When a man abuses a woman
Verbally or otherwise
It's the woman who feels the pain
And her children who have to cry.

When a man abuses a woman
We often wonder why
Did his father do this to his mother
And he was the one to cry.

When a man abuses a woman
He seldom tells her he loves her
The main reason is
He thinks that he's above her

When a man abuses a woman
Why can't she seem to see
He most likely will never change
And that's reality

Why do we allow ourselves
To be subjected to such abuse
To stay in such a relationship is like tightening the noose

When a man abuses a woman
She's the one who deserves much better
She needs a man, who will treat her as his treasure

A woman is beautiful inside and out
And should not sell herself short, without a doubt
A man who says he loves her
Will have her in his plans
And because he is a man
He will never abuse a woman.

22

"He Hurt Me"

He hurt me
But what was I to do
He was no stranger to me
Yet look what he put me through.
He hurt me
I didn't know what to say
He stolen something from me
And he wasn't going away.
He hurt me
When my mother wasn't home
The sad part is
I was often home alone.
He hurt me
Her boyfriend, her husband
Whoever he was to be
He often did things to me
Things little girls shouldn't have to see.
He hurt me
He did things I shouldn't have known about
Yet, my mother wouldn't even put him out.
He hurt me
The things he did were wrong
Now I am finally, trying to move on.
But it hurts me
That he walks free today
Never to face charges
Not even for one day.
We tell our children
Not to talk to strangers
But they aren't always the ones
Who present them with the danger
He hurt me...

"My Sistah's Keeper"

I'm not my sistah's keeper
But that night I should have been
And saved her from herself
And what happened in the end.

I should have been her keeper
And this story never told
Had I known what would have happened
Because her liquor, she could not hold.

This brotha was suited and booted
What they call buttafly
There was no doubt in my mind
Why he had caught her eye.

They say don't judge a book by its cover
Cause its sometimes good to read
But something about this brotha
He had something up his sleeve.

Some think it's easier, to go with the flow
But it's not always smart, cause you just never know
Don't let his words fool you, into playing it unsafe
While he leaves you something special, in your sacred place.

He was gentle, meticulous and hit it just right
He worked it so good, she wanted it every night
Not once did she question what his status was
Nor did she suggest the use of a glove.

She should have listened to the grapevine
And what it had to say
Cause what this brotha shared
Would take her breath away.

When the grapevine rang
She didn't pick up the phone
This brotha came at her foul
And really did her wrong.

Rumor had it; he was on the down low
Fresh out of prison, hiding his life from the row
At churches and clubs, like a wolf on the prowl
Now connecting with numerous women is his lifestyle.

He led her to believe, that she was the queen
But it was the other way around or so it seems.

I'm not my sistah's keeper
But that night I should have been
Cause look at this mess that she's caught up in.

Now her world is turned upside down
Cause a brotha with aids, came sniffin around
Know your status and know his too
Make sure to use condoms as part of what you do.

He may not want to, but don't leave it to the man
Demand he use a condom and be firm on your stand

One can only take so much
When it's their life, that has been touched
Since she felt there was nothing else to do
She killed him and herself too.

I'm not my sistah's keeper
But that night I should have been
And since I couldn't save her
I'll try and save a friend.

So always use a condom even if he's buttafly
Cause you have a responsibility
To yourself and your quality of life!

"What's Right"

Where does the responsibility lie
It doesn't just drop from the sky.
Take responsibility for yourself
Then you can look at someone else.
Do what's right, when no one's around
Then you know, your foundation is sound.
Simply do what's required of you
Cuz no one, can take that from you.
So lead by example, whenever you can
And with that, you'll be honorable in your stand.
With people, some do what's right
And others do wrong
But don't let those be the values
That you drive home.

"Wes"

You came in and impacted our lives
In a way, you may not know
And it breaks our hearts
That it was your time to go.

Our love for you, grew each and every day
And we're still accepting that it was god's way
We know you won't have to suffer anymore
And prayers for you to stay would've been what we ask for.

The gentle giant that we will truly miss
The one who would do anything
To go out on the creek to fish.

It's that deep and raspy voice
That I dare fail to mention
It was something special about it
That commanded our attention.

So we know you're in a better place
Never again having pain to face.
So we say, see you later
Cause god's plans for you are greater.

So go to your heavenly home to rest
And we'll see you again one day.
Our memories will last forever
And never go away.

So every tear we cry is absorbed by the twinkles in your eye.
As you watch over us
From your great view up in the sky.

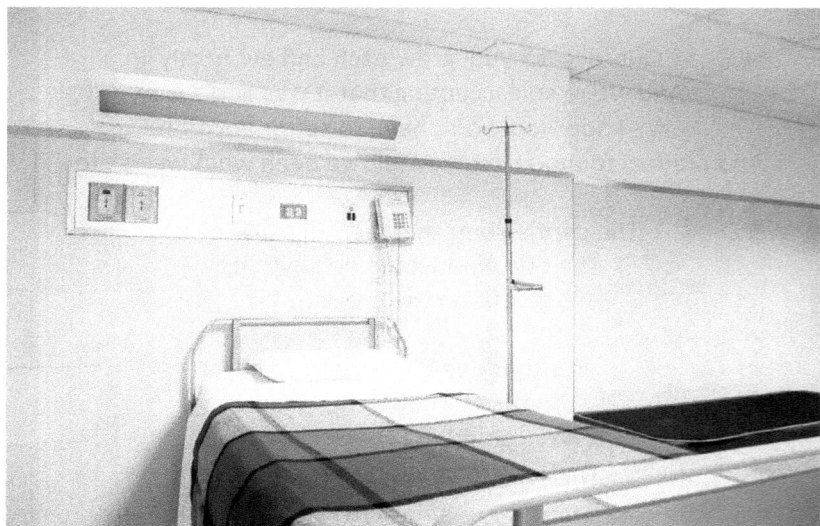

"Mother"

There is no loss
Like that of a loved one
And the loss of a mother
Is a most devastating one.
There are no words
To soothe how you feel
It's just a matter of time
Before you can heal.
Remember the good times
And carry them with you
Having those in your heart
Will surely get you through.
You know that she's in a better place
Never again, a worry to face.

"Father"

A father is a man
Who is there regardless
One who can love you
Through times that are the hardest.

You know what it was like, for your father not to be there
So how can you do this to me
You know it isn't fair.

I needed my father, to teach me to be a man
Because of your absence
I'll struggle to understand.

No matter what the reason
You left me to stand alone.
But with the help of my mother
I know I'll turn out strong.

As strong as she can make me
From her point of view.
But it would have been much easier
To learn it from you.

Thanks for helping to give me life
That's all I thank you for
And maybe one day
I'll be thankful for much more.

"Loss"

A sense of loss is what they feel
Look what they've been through with this ordeal
A disaster, that compares to no other
It separated husbands from wives and children from mothers.

A strength will come, because they survived.
And after the hurt, they're still alive
Some lost everything, except the clothes on their backs
We can't begin to imagine, a loss like that.

Many will regroup and get back on track
But others won't ever recover or even bounce back.
There are no words, to take the pain away
It's a thing called time that will take its place.

We hope they will stay strong in their beliefs
And not get consumed in their grief
Try to dust off the clouds covered in gray
And keep the good memories to guide the way.

Our prayers go our to all of the survivors
In their time of need.
Helping where we can, so they can proceed.

Survivors...
Remember the smiles
And the little things that make life worthwhile.

Hurricane Katrina
August 2005

"Beautiful"

You're beautiful
And special in every way
You're beautiful my daughter
And I love you more each day
Being beautiful and special
Can lead you on the way
And always remember
You're beautiful in every way
You're beautiful, intelligent, and really truly sweet
You have a lot to offer
And it makes you so complete
You're a leader
Who often speaks out loud
So remember your beauty
Stands out in a crowd
You're beautiful Charniece!

Love Mom

"Her Confidence"

Although it shows in my stroll
I try to control, the beauty I behold.
It takes very little to show it
Cause my smile and glow fit.
See, my hips tend to sway
When the brothas, look my way.
As the moisture starts to ascend
It highlights the flawlessness of my skin.
While I wear a devilish grin
As my thoughts, revert to sin.
Since black doesn't seem to crack
I tend to cut a brotha slack
Because of the sway of my hips and the arch in my back
I have an overwhelming tendency to attract.
All types of men young and old
It's just an aura that I hold
That exudes deep from my soul.
Its part of my confidence, or so I'm told.

"Forbidden"

How can you ask forgiveness, from someone you don't know

For thoughts that are in your head, that you can't seem to let go.

Having feelings for someone, that you really aren't supposed to

But longing for them, in everything you do.

No one can tell you, if your feelings are right or wrong

And you tend not to listen and just move right along.

How can you ask forgiveness, for something you haven't done

Yet the thoughts that fill your head bring you so much fun.

A taste of forbidden fruit is why we are how we are today

So think twice before you act, that's all I have to say!

"Friendship First"

I just wanted to let you know
How you make me feel
Your smile brightens up my day
It chases my blues away.

I really don't know why
I feel the way I do
It's just something about you
Your eyes say it too.

Good looks, intelligence
And a silent charm
Makes me want to hold you
Gently in my arms

I hope I'm not being
Too forward
I'm usually very shy
But there's something about you
That says you're a nice guy

So let's be friends first
And see where that leads us
Because intimacy before friendship
Is simply not enough.

"Enjoy the Ride"

When I met you, You looked into my eyes

Then my feelings, I could no longer hide.

The vibe I felt coming from you

Made me more comfortable, then I'm use to

You wanted to search the depths of my soul

At least, those were the words that I was told

We explored our options in a few different ways

Through our conversations and the games we played.

Now let's enjoy the time that we share and not get caught up if

we dare

Let's just enjoy the ride for what it is worth and hope that no one

will get hurt

No regrets for what we do, we will keep those things between me

and you

We learned from all those we met before, leaving our minds open

and free to explore.

Enjoy the Ride!

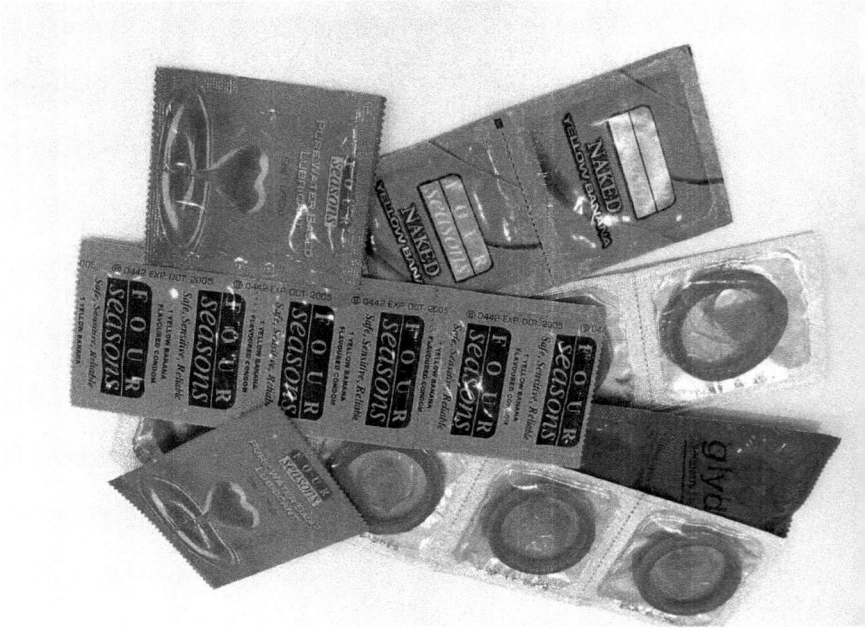

"Protect Yourself"

Wrap it up, that's what they say
Wrap it up before you play
I guess I thought it couldn't happen to me
I was with one man and tested regularly
I didn't think this could happen to me
But, I wasn't too knowledgeable about HIV
I thought he was a good man, because he was good to me
And he hadn't spent time in the penitentiary
No alcohol or drugs intravenously
Wrap it up and don't be a fool, who thinks using condoms isn't cool
He was a good lover and that could have been a clue
That I should protect myself in all that I do.
So have him wrap it up, take it from me
If I had only insisted, I would remain disease free
Wrap it up to save your life, if you don't think once
You better think twice
Before I knew it, things had changed for me
I was pregnant and carrying HIV
So wrap it up, cause that's how it has to be
Because it's no Joke getting HIV
Wrap it up!

"Can't Commit"

You say you love me with some of your actions

But often times there's a distraction

How am I supposed to feel

While I question if your love is real

You say I'm your homie, lover, friend

And you'll be there till the end.

Why not commit to me

Show me the man you proclaim to be

Is the grass greener on the other side

Or

Is this your way to run and hide?

Commit to no one, it's safer this way

So you can play the games you play

Commit to me or someone else

Or

Better yet, just check yourself

Because you can't commit

"A Mothers Love"

You said I turned my back on you

What else was I was supposed to do

Tough love for me is something new

Especially when it comes to you

I stood behind you, day after day

And you did things to turn me away

You chose her over me

Maybe that's how it had to be

You took that stand to be with her

And left your home, I didn't concur

Only because you weren't ready

I tried to guide you and keep you steady

As your mother, I've always stood by you

Forgiveness is something you must want to do

I pray each day, that this will mend

And we can be mother and son again.

"Middle Child"

Because you were born second
Not last and not first
You may often feel like it's a curse
It's Not.
You're special in every way
But often I don't find the time to say
I couldn't love you more if you were born again today.
You have a special smile
That takes away the anger
And
You have a special gift for befriending those called strangers.
You're smart, talented and full of energy
And often find the good in those who seem like enemies.
Being in the middle is hard from time to time
So you'll learn what you will and leave the rest behind.
You have the ability to empower those younger than you
So be strong big brother, cause your little brother looks up to you
Guide him in a positive way, because he will follow in your footsteps
someday.
You may have been the second born
But you're number one in every way.
For Richard

"How Cancer Made Me Feel in a Relationship"

I was in a place
Darker than any hole
Trying to get out
Wasn't even my goal.
I stayed there motionless
As things started to unfold
Not knowing that it was affecting
Me as a whole.
My mental and physical
simply went to sleep
And I was unable to fight back
Cause I was just too weak.
Stuck in a situation
That I didn't try to get out of
Simply because, he used the word love
Then one day
It all hit the fan
I saw the true colors
Of a frightened man
He had a void
That he needed to be filled
He did what he thought i needed
But it wasn't real.
See you can't love another
Before you love yourself
So that's when I realized
That I was top shelf!
I didn't need an extra burden in my life
Being with someone when it wasn't right.
Be careful what you ask for
Cause you may or may not get it
And in the end
You are no longer down with it.
The sun is shinning now
And I can see the light.
Staying in survival mode
It is fight or flight.
See I am a strong woman, again able to stand
Cause I know god has for me a bigger plan.

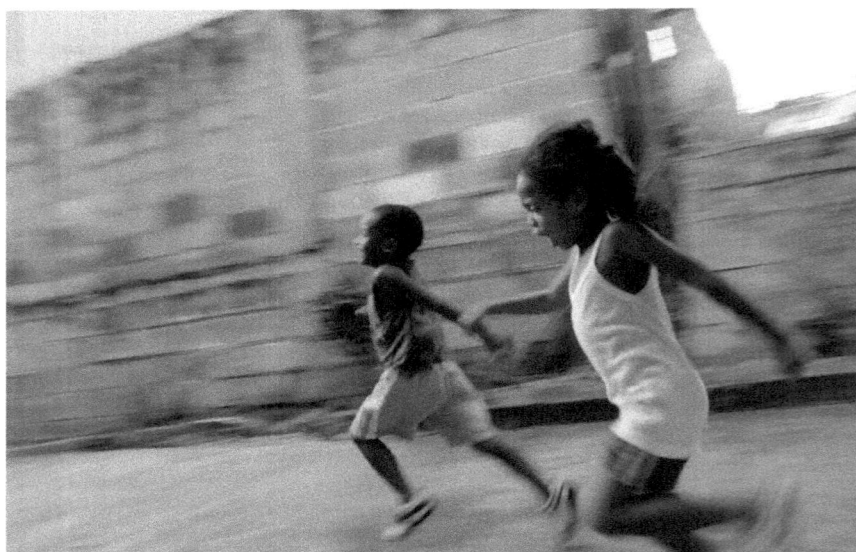

"Babay's Kids"

(Inspired by Robin Harris's comedic skit Bebe's Kids)
Babay's kids, what can I say
You see them, each and every day
A little rough and often smart
But Baby's kids need a fresh start
They had to learn things on their own
Cause Babays' mama's never home
She leaves them little food to eat
Then she goes and hits the streets
She goes for drugs that call her name
Even with kids, she has no shame
Babay wasn't there and the kids aren't to blame
But what happened to them, was a down right shame
She left them home alone, days at a time
Knowing good and well, it's a crime
They wear a label, earned from her name
And they wear it proud just the same
Its not their fault, that they turned out bad
They only worked with what they had
One day, one of Babay's kids slipped and fell
And a concerned neighbor was forced to tell.
Now Babay's kids are the ones to pay, Cause Now Babay is gone away
Babay's kids just couldn't see, It's just sad
But...Babay's a JUNKIE!!

"What's It Like?"

I can't pretend to understand what it's like to be a man

My perception may be mildly skewed

But this is from what I've viewed

Being a black man young or old

You never know how your life unfolds

The killing of each other or being killed by the police

Should be a worry, you have the least

The influx of violence that plaques our streets

Makes it hard, for your goals to reach

Knowledge is power so they say

So we need more black men in college today

Our strong men should be scholars in the making

The education is there, ready for the taking

Don't be a statistic, leave the stereotypes behind

So those that follow will have a solid guideline.

"Infatuation"

Infatuation is to fall foolishly in love

When there is only one person

You're always thinking of

You want to know him and him to know you

To be there as a friend and a lover too

To make him happy when he is blue

Let him know your feelings for him are true

Infatuation can go on and on forever

And

Suddenly end very swift and very clever

"How Many Times"

How many times did I yell at those kids
Because they did what they did
How many times did I say No
And turn around and let them go
How many times did I work late
To make sure there was food on their plates
How many times did I sit down and read
So that my children would succeed
How many times did I go without
Because I love them without a doubt
How many times did I kneel to pray
To keep them from going astray
How many times did I shower to buffer my cries
So that they didn't see the tears in my eyes
How many times did I tell them I love them
I hope it was enough to sustain them.

"Six Weeks"

As she lays quietly, I don't know what to say
She's resting more peacefully than any other day
See, she's always been my rock, my Johnny on the spot
Always on the move, like her bottoms Hot.
She was the life of the party, wherever she goes
She has touched more people, in more ways than she knows
How dare I be smug and give her an attitude
There were even times when I was a little rude.
Her job as a mother is a thankless one
Where the word thank you, very seldom comes
But I always acknowledge her, because she is the one
The one who gave birth to me and made each day a life
She made sure I had all that I needed, although through sacrifice.
A mother's love is like no other
So I would never place anyone above her
As she lays quietly without a word to say
Six weeks in this bed is where she lay
I talk to her, read to her and let the music play
All of this in hopes she will awaken one day
Because of her, I have a strength that I can't even explain
And the love that I have for her, no one could obtain.
I inhale and I smell the fragrance that she sometimes wears
I want her to open her eyes, so she can see I'm there.
But her body lays motionlessly, in need of time to heal
Yet my heart feels heavy, because it seems so unreal.
Six weeks have passed
And fate sealed the deal.

"Remission"

I often reminisce on the things I've been through

How grateful I am, from those things I grew.

So lucky, Not to hold a grudge

Cause they tend to weigh you down

Joyful, for the smile I wear and not a constant frown.

See, I'd get a check up

Each and Every year

But this one year, I was faced with an unthinkable fear.

One that lead me to believe

That this earth I would leave

But because my doctor was good and caught it fast

With Surgery and treatment, it was a thing of the past.

So with God's permission, I am now in remission

I may have to take medication for the rest of my days

But it beats the alternative of lying dead in a grave.

Remission!

DX:DEC 2012/Jan 2013
Surgery April 1, 2013
Thyroid cancer

"Ungrateful Child"

Your mother raised you and she did it alone

She may have given you too much and entitlements lead you wrong

You went down a path that you weren't ready for

And your actions, got you put out the door

Since actions have consequences that you couldn't see

Yet when they were presented, suddenly you see clearly

It's a bitter pill to swallow with bumps and bruises along the way

And hard lessons are learned that may help you some day

You only get one mother, who'll support you like no other

Cherish her for as long as she lives

Cause no one will sacrifice and gives as she gives

Honor your Mother!

"Settling Into Normal"

Now the dust has settled, I know not what I do
I can no longer function, not like I use to
I force myself to go on, each and every day
But it's really hard now, cause I just want to lay
Lay my head on my pillow and not get out of bed
So I guess it's not as easily done, as it is said.
My heart is hurting, from the space you left behind
And my memories will have to fill it, along with some time.
Some don't know the struggle of my day
Yet I try to remain strong and tuck the pain away
Although some see me, the sadness in my eyes
Others try to comfort me, as my cries I try to hide.
I'm in my emotions and don't know how to feel
I try to remember prayers, as a way to help me heal
I also find solace
In knowing that you're not here mentally, but spiritually
Thanks mommie for continuing to watch over me.

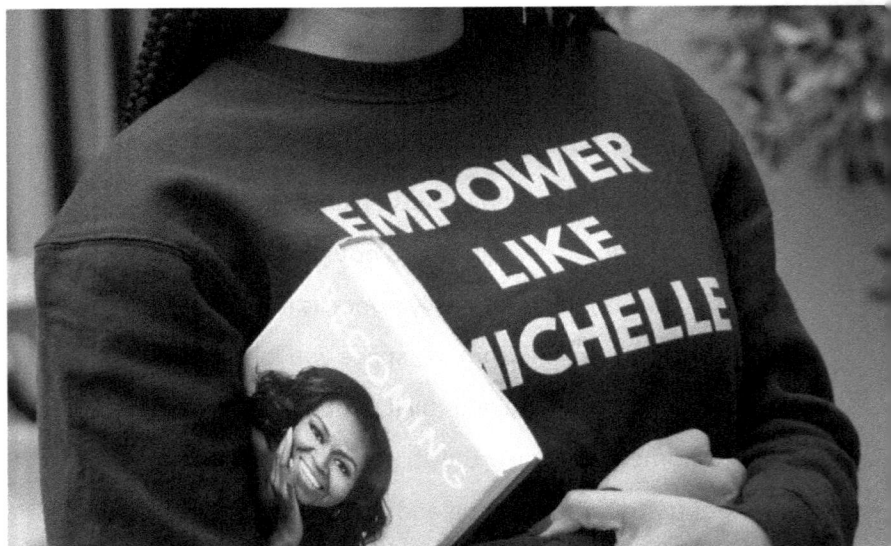

"Know Your Worth"

Don't believe you deserve less than the best
Don't allow your situation to cause you stress
Don't settle for any type of abuse
Because if you do, it's like tightening the noose.
Nothing is harder for family and friends
Then when a young life comes to an end
Simply because you didn't walk away
Thinking its love and deciding to stay.
When you look in the mirror
Beauty is all you should see
Not reflections of what you've done
Or what you're expected to be.
You're beautiful, smart, intelligent and strong
You're meant to be cherished and not done wrong
First, love yourself, like no one else will
It's all about you and how you feel.
No one should hold your happiness
In the palms of their hand
So on your two feet, you must take a stand
Know who you are and know your worth
Don't let anyone cause you to hurt
Cause no love is worth bumps and bruises
No one wins, everyone loses.

"Doing Business"

Why can't we just simply get along
Why do we always look for what's wrong
We can't come together in unity and be strong
Because it's just to hard for us to get along.
Why, can't we even patron one another
Giving a helping hand to ones we call brother
We're far too busy, stepping on the next man
Finding it difficult to just lend a helping hand.
Providing and sharing information to help one grow
Is a concept, we just don't know
It's always a doggie dog world
Nothing but venom and hatred we hurl
See, when we walk into a business, were treated down right rude
Barely a greeting and much attitude
If we tend to go to another store
They overcompensate, because our money they want to make
Cause if you come back again, you may tell a friend
And that's how their profits will ascend.
We need to band together, so we can see each other grow
You may never know, just how far we can go.
No matter the color, greet each person with a smile.
Treat them like their money means something
And their business is worthwhile.
Don't let them walk out, feeling defeated
Cause your treatment of them, make them fell depleted.
Always remember they work hard for theirs too
And they can spend their hard earned money
Wherever they choose.

"All Grown Up"

Always wanting to grow up, before we needed to
Never knowing the responsibility
That's in store for you
We lived each day
As though tomorrow didn't exist
Not ready for all of the turns and twist
Playing hide-n-go get it
Before we knew what get it was
Now ever so cautious, in the use of a glove
Knowing what penicillin cured back in the day
It's not a chance you'd take now, cause with your life you'd pay
As time went past, faster than the speed of light
Years later, you'd think we'd get it right
Family has taken precedence over hanging with our friends
Now holding down a job and paying bills
Is a means to an end
Some knew the career path that would make the most money
Others still let their hormones guide them to the honey
What a dollar could buy back then, Today can't buy at all
Cause now you find yourself robbing Peter to pay Paul
And here we stand with our good mental health
Some still playing the Lotto, others working for their wealth
Above all else, we're truly blessed to see
A black man become president, changing the face of history
We're All Grown Up!

"If I Could"

If I could, I'd celebrate your life

Simply because, that is what you'd like

If I could, I'd dry the tears I cry for you

Those I shed to help to get me through

If I could, I would smile each day

If it would help, the pain to go away

If I could, I wouldn't be so sad

Because, I know the life we had

If I could, I would free my mind

Knowing where you are and that you'll be just fine

If I could, I'd make sure to repent my sins

So, I'd be sure to see you once again

If I could, I'd say one more time, I love you

I miss you and I enjoyed our time.

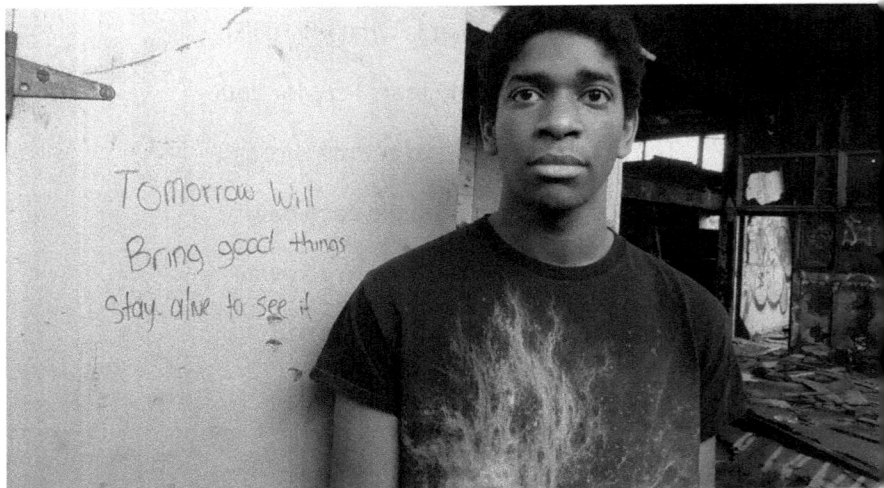

"Not the Way!"

When you're depressed and feeling sad
Try to remember things aren't that bad.
When you're feeling really low
And you can't seem to get through the day
Suicide is not the way.
Although sometimes you want to throw in the towel
Stand up and let out a piercing howl.
Because we sometimes have to vent
And this is indeed true
Just remember the best thing to do.
This action may provide a relief for you
But those left behind will hurt too.
You only have one life to live
And there are many things you can give
The gift of love to family and friends
Not letting the hard times do you in
Figure it out, because you can
Cause the man upstairs has a greater plan.
Suicide is not the way
And a few words could make a difference between Go or Stay!

"Freak"

You brought me to a place
I didn't think I'd be
You allowed me to explore
The freak inside of me
We ventured into areas
I didn't think I'd see.
You took out the time
To really get to know me.
Because of some things
That you instilled in me
I can no longer be as reserved
As I proclaimed to be.
I know there are some things
That you really want to show me
So bring em on and continue to explore me.
I only offer myself to you
Knowing you'll keep me safe
In all that you say and do
As I cherish your embrace.
So for you, I am a freak
And there are no limits to what you and I can do
You brought out the freak in me
And I did the same for you.

"Cry No More"

Cry No more
I don't want you to be sad
Just remember the joyous times we had
Remember, how this all came to be
Cause, God has bigger plans for me
So don't shed another tear
Cause I'm still right here.
I'll be watching over you
And all the things you do
So honor me, as I know you will
No matter how bad you may often feel
Cause we will meet again one day
Where all the Angels gather to play!

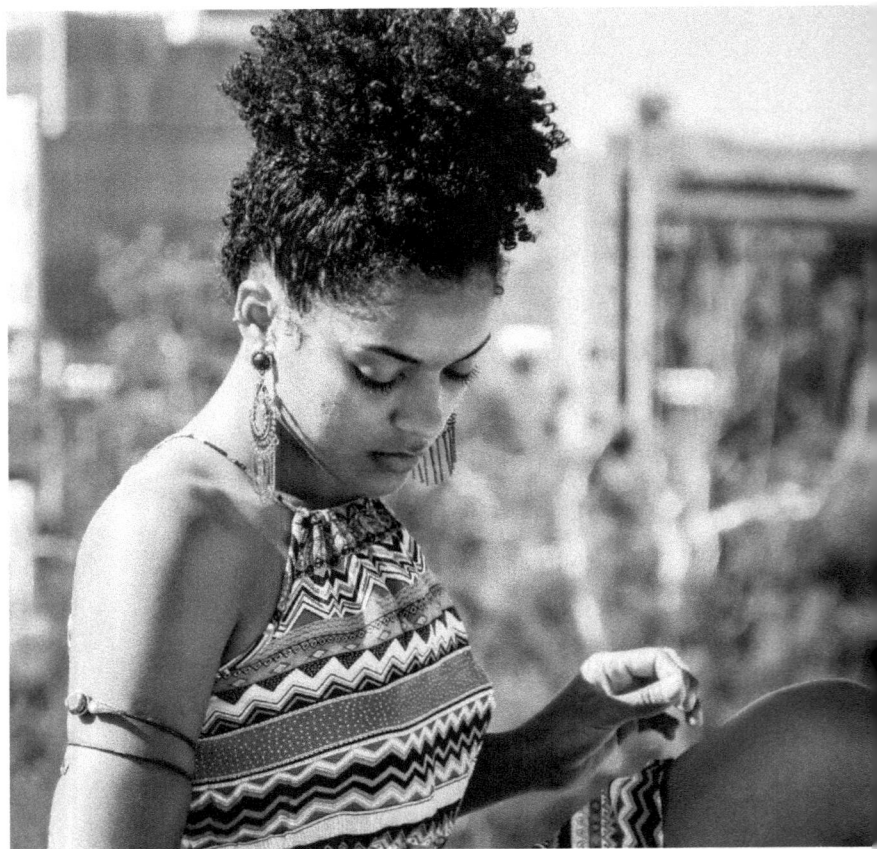

"Stood Up"

When you're stood up
You wonder why
You wonder if you should laugh or cry.
Maybe he wants you
But is still unsure
He wants first to know his feelings are secure.
Prior to placing his love in your hands
He wants to know you and understand
You tell him your feelings, which are oh so true
But doubt still fills him like they do.
You want to love him and him to love you
You could give him good love, if you had the chance to.
Too much love and very little play
Has made your lives go separate ways.
You think one day, he'll come around
And you wait patiently without a sound.
Friends you'll be for now
Cause you'll try to get his love somehow
As long as he doesn't wait too long
And someone else comes along.

"Revamp it!"

Don't be so quick to buck authority
Remember you are considered the minority
Things aren't set up for you to win
So you have to give things a different spin
Don't let them provoke you, from how you were taught
That's how some of you end up getting caught
Caught up in an ugly Malay
Placed in a cell, where they want you to stay
The system isn't set up for your brown skin
And it's a definite means to an end
There are times when you know that you are wrong
And then those actions are ones you must own
Other times they are wrong too
Going to the extreme in what it is they do
The law is something that is supposed to keep you safe
But the actions of some has put fear in its place
The kind of fear that insights fight or flight
Even when you know it's not right
Revamp it, Revamp it, Revamp it
There shouldn't be privilege for some and degradation for others
Treatment should be the same and all people equally covered.

"Potential"

There shouldn't be any goal that is unattainable

If you put your mind to it

If you stay focused and determined

I know that you can do it

Don't let the little things

Stand in your way

Make sure you are resourceful

In every single way

Make moves and do it with purpose

Cause the best laid plans

Helps your goals to rise to the surface.

"Drama"

We try to avoid drama in our life
But if there was no drama
Things wouldn't be quite right.
From the baby daddy
To the baby Mama
There is usually some type of drama.
The rent can't get paid
If you don't go to work
When your partner is caught cheating
Someone ends up hurt
Your spirit can not be fed
If you don't go to church
When no condom is used
It's a woman who gives birth
Everyone has a little drama in their life
A boyfriend, a husband, a girlfriend or a wife
The type of drama that causes tension
The kind of tension we try to avoid or even mention.
Being the mother, maid, doctor or even the cook
Putting up with things, that you never should have took.
Why can't we all try and get along
Cause if things are going smoothly
We feel that something wrong.
Sometimes there is more drama than one cares to know
From the top of our heads, to the bottom of our toes.
Drama!

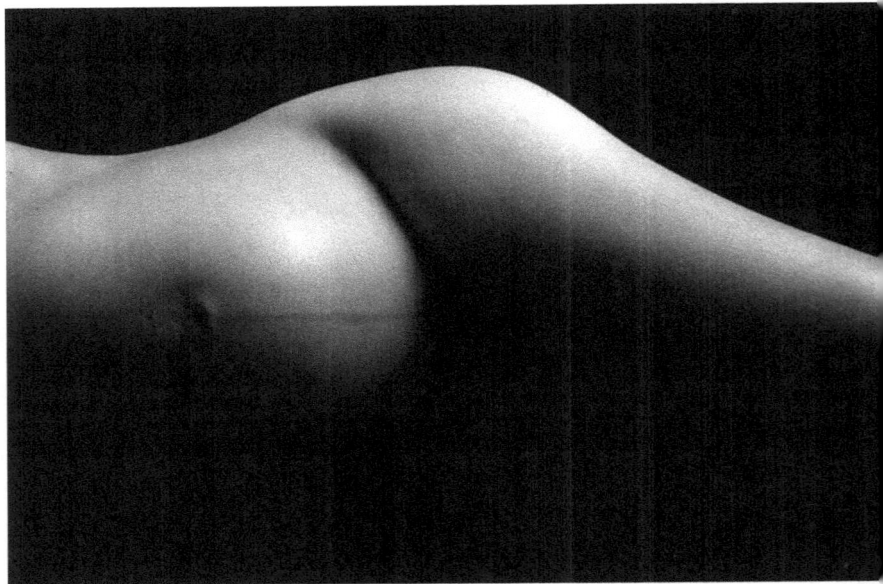

"My Choice"

This man I've chosen not to marry

Yet his child I chose to carry

Next time marry I must do

Or

No more children for you know who

Kids are sweet and a joy I'm sure

But

I can't see two or more.

Financially you can't win

From the day their born, the pimping begins

They will always be there, you must face

And

They grow at such a rapid pace.

So, now for me contraceptives win

And after this baby, I'm giving in.

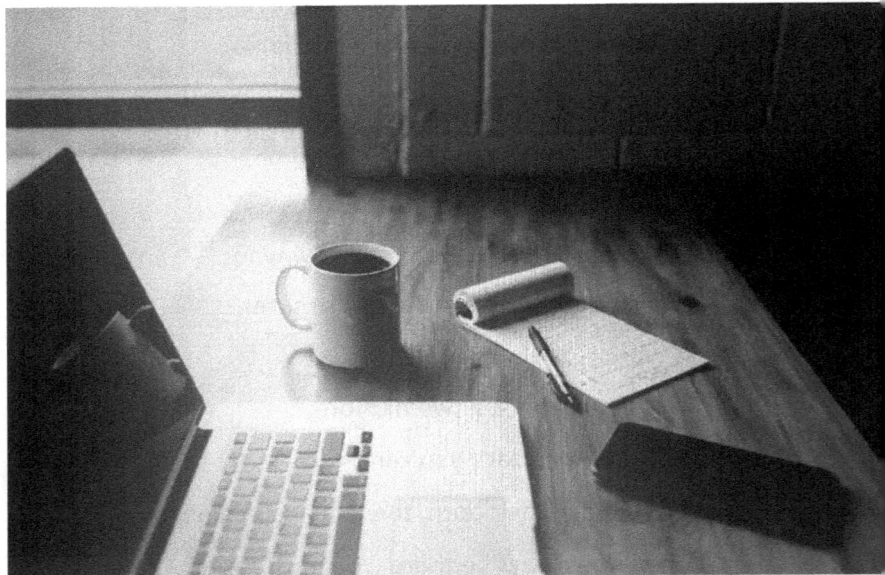

"I Write"

I often write to clear my mind
I often write to pass the time
I love to write either way
I write to chase the blues away
I know my gift is special to me
So I often vent through poetry.
I write...
So that I can express an emotion
And share something real
And in my writing, it reflects emotions that I feel
Sometimes I write because my words I can't verbally articulate
So writing seems to flow and fits right into place.
I write because that is all I have even done
It's nothing like work, it's a lot like fun.

"Joy"

We all will grow tired

And need to get some rest

And what better place for us to nest

But in the arms of the Lord, in heaven at best.

No need for anyone to be sad

She closes her eyes, because she has to

But looks down from above

And watches over you.

There will be no more pain or even worry

No need to go through her day in a hurry.

She is now with the man upstairs

Where she will remain, In our hearts and our prayers.

She has secured her place in line

But don't think you've seen her for the last time

This is only the beginning to what some call the end

But our time will come too

And we'll see her again.

www.ingramcontent.com/pod-product-compliance
Lightning Source LLC
Chambersburg PA
CBHW071147090426
42736CB00012B/2257